Getting the Most Out of Teaching With Newspapers

by Rebecca Olien

SCHOLASTIC
PROFESSIONAL BOOKS

NEW YORK • TORONTO • LONDON • AUCKLAND • SYDNEY
MEXICO CITY • NEW DELHI • HONG KONG • BUENOS AIRES

To all my students
who have made teaching and learning
so much fun.

Special thanks to Scholastic News Zone editors,
Rebecca Bonder, Steven Ehrenberg, and Suzanne Freeman.

Regulations regarding printing material for use from newspapers and from the Internet are not always clear.
Talk with your local newspaper to learn about printing articles from the paper and their Web site for classroom use.

Cover design by Josué Castilleja
Cover illustration by Steve Cox
Interior design by Solutions by Design, Inc.
Interior illustrations by Claudine Gévry
Illustration p. 47 by Kate Flanagan
ISBN 0-439-22256-7

CONTENTS

INTRODUCTION

WHAT'S BLACK AND WHITE AND READ ALL OVER?

Newspapers, we hope. Statistics indicate, however, that because of television and video games, young adults are reading less news than ever. To get kids into the act of reading the news—and reading it critically!—we can show our students that newspapers provide information relevant to their lives. With thoughtful, hands-on teaching, we can demonstrate how newspapers inform, educate, and entertain us and help us interpret and influence our world.

WHY USE NEWSPAPERS?

Newspapers communicate high-interest current events to the public. Helping students learn to read and enjoy newspapers when they are young encourages them to become lifelong readers and learners with a more global outlook. When the newspaper becomes a part of students' everyday lives, their curiosity about the world is heightened. They not only gain a better perspective on life in places other than their homes, but their ability to understand themselves and show compassion for others increases.

Teaching with newspapers also promotes critical-thinking skills. Activities guide students to classify, summarize, and organize information from articles, so they can increase their comprehension as they read for information and research to learn more.

Newspapers are easy to obtain and provide a wealth of information and resources at minimal cost or for free. (See Quick Tips on page 5 for suggestions about obtaining newspapers for class use.)

HOW TO USE THIS BOOK

The activities in this book are divided into three parts. Part One, Getting to Know the Newspaper, provides games and activities to help students become comfortable using the newspaper and familiar with its language. Part Two, Using the Newspaper as a Learning Tool, offers ideas on how to use the newspaper to make connections across the curriculum. Part Three, Creating Classroom Newspapers, explains a method for starting a classroom paper. Each section begins with tips to help make lessons run smoothly and to make learning more complete.

The following extra activities and applications appear throughout the book:

> **Extensions** carry the activity farther with advanced students,
> or can be used with the class if time and interest allow.

> **Critical Thinking Questions** can be used as prompts for
> discussions or journal writing.

> **Web Links** provide ideas for Internet Web sites and help you
> integrate technology into your curriculum.

PART ONE

GETTING TO KNOW THE NEWSPAPER

Quick Tips: *Managing newspapers in the classroom*

NEWSPAPER ARTICLE COLLECTIONS

- With students' interests in mind (animals, sports, local events, famous people), collect related articles and photos to display on a poster or bulletin board.

- As students begin to take notice, encourage them to bring in their own articles to share and post.

NEWSPAPER STAND

- Keep a collection of different newspaper titles in the classroom in a special area, using wooden crates as benches, tables, and shelves to hold the papers.

- When they go out of town, encourage students to bring back nonlocal newspapers for the newsstand.

- Keep newspaper puzzles and activities at the stand to encourage students to practice skills they've learned in class.

- Hang newspapers over clotheslines for students to take down and read.

OBTAINING NEWSPAPERS

- Inform your local newspaper that you are a teacher and need copies for class use; most local press companies provide discounted rates for educators. Some publishers have education coordinators who can give advice about the cheapest way to obtain papers, as well as provide other services such as teaching materials, classroom visits, and tours of the news and printing facilities.

- Ask parents and staff to donate their newspapers. Churches, local businesses, and libraries are often happy to set out a box for newspaper collections.

MANAGING AND ORGANIZING

- Make articles easier to read by enlarging them on a copy machine.

- Laminate articles about popular topics so they last longer. This saves time, as many articles are appropriate to use year after year.

- Staple pages together along the folded edge of each section so that the large sheets of newspaper are easier to handle

- To keep activities neater, use glue sticks instead of liquid glue, and provide hand wipes to clean off black ink.

- For reference, label articles with title of paper, section, page, and date.

USING NEWS ON THE WEB

Want to share an article with the class, but don't have access to a copy? The Internet can help! Many newspapers have Web sites that post summaries or entire articles, and may allow you to to search for back issues. Accessing newspapers from major metropolitan areas (for example, *The New York Times*) enables you to read with your class several consecutive articles about an ongoing event from one source or find and compare related articles from different newspapers.

For kid-friendly breaking news written at an upper-grade reading level, check out **Scholastic News Zone** at **http://teacher.scholastic.com**. This site offers a variety of articles and projects for many ability levels. The content complements news features in Scholastic's Classroom Magazines, such as *Scholastic News 3*, *Scholastic News 4*, and *Junior Scholastic*.

Scholastic News Zone at http://teacher.scholastic.com

Top News displays current high interest articles that students may read individually or as a class. Suggested Web sites provide students with research opportunities that also help them build technology skills.

Special Issues allows your students to explore many areas of the news in depth and provides lesson helpers for teachers.

Games and Quizzes offers short activities as well as contests that spark students' interest in the news.

Pop Zone is an age-appropriate area where students can catch up on news about their favorite celebrities.

Vote Now encourages students to express their opinions about high-interest current-events issues and see how their peers across the nation stand on these issues.

Teacher Tips guides you through the News Zone hassle-free!

Scholastic Classroom magazines are available on-line at the Scholastic News Zone site or by calling 1-800-SCHOLASTIC.

NUMBER THE SPOT

Learning to identify and locate the parts of the paper helps students navigate the paper and provides the class with a common vocabulary when referring to the sections and features during activities and discussions.

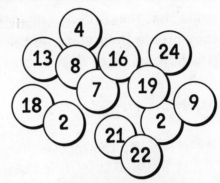

What to Do

1. Go over the parts of the paper and introduce vocabulary. Hand out the glossary for students to follow as you explain and show examples with a newspaper.

2. Pass out newspapers and a set of circle stickers, numbered 1–24, to each pair of students.

3. Explain to students that they are to locate and mark with a sticker each different part of the paper.

4. Call out the following newspaper parts one at a time, writing each item on the board before saying the next. A suggested order follows.

   1. section C, 2. section A, 3. section B, 4. index, 5. classified ads, 6. comics, 7. weather map, 8. local news, 9. stock market report, 10. movie schedule, 11. editorials, 12. TV schedule, 13. world news, 14. entertainment section, 15. masthead, 16. cutline, 17. byline, 18. dateline, 19. ear on the first page, 20. flag, 21. filler, 22. gutter, 23. hard news story, 24. feature

5. Students place each numbered sticker (e.g., #1 for section C) on the correct part of the paper.

6. After all students have completed the assignment, have them compare the placement of their stickers. Go over results and questions.

Materials

(for each student or pair)

☐ Newspaper Glossary (page 62)
☐ 24 removable circle stickers numbered 1–24
☐ 1 newspaper

. . . .

CHALLENGE

. . . .

Invite students to create an acrostic using the glossary and the letters in the word *news* or *newspaper*. The crossing words do not have to begin with a letter of the vertical word.

```
b y l i n e
    e a r
    w i r e s e r v i c e
r e l e a s e
```

When students are finished, share results in class and have students give definitions aloud for words that they have used to create the acrostics. Or have them create a crossword puzzle on graph paper and write clues for the terms that fit in each space.

SHUFFLING

Students learn to appreciate the decision-making and teamwork skills that go into organizing a newspaper, skills that they will find necessary when they create their class newspaper (Part Three, page 56).

What to Do

1. Review the content of each section of the paper, asking questions that will help students sort and classify articles, such as, *What kinds of articles appear on the front page? What kind of news story belongs in the local (metro) section? In the international section? How about the business section?*

2. Divide the class into editorial teams of three or four students.

3. Have each team decide cooperatively how the articles and ads should be organized on their newspaper dummy based on similarities in content, newsworthiness, and subject matter. Make sure they label each page of the dummy with the title of a major section that you want them to focus on, such as front page, national, international, local, business, sports, and so on.

4. Allow teams to glue articles onto the dummy, using a marker to add section headings, banners, a masthead, and an index.

5. Share newspapers in class.

Materials

(for each team)
- marker
- 2 sheets of blank newsprint paper folded into an 8-page newspaper dummy
- copies of 20 or more articles and ads from different sections of the newspaper
- original copy of the newspaper for reference

EXTENSION

Editorial Choices

If each group is given copies of the same articles, conduct a follow-up discussion where students explain reasons for their choice of organization. Student choices might also be compared with a copy of the original paper, intact, to see how their editorial choices compare with those of the editors.

NEWSPAPER SCAVENGER HUNT

Working in teams, students race to put their newspaper navigational skills to the test. The Number the Spot activity (page 7) can help students sharpen their familiarity with the newspaper terminology they will encounter in this activity. For extra support, distribute the Newspaper Glossary (page 62) for students' reference.

What to Do

1. Divide the class into teams of three or four students.

2. Distribute copies of Newspaper Scavenger Hunt (page 10) and review unfamiliar terms.

3. Explain that each team will be given 20 minutes to find as many items on the sheet as possible. Emphasize that each team needs to work cooperatively to be successful.

4. Direct students to cut out and glue each item they find to their team's sheet of paper and to label it with the name of the item, the section from which it came, and the page number. This will allow you to check the accuracy of their search.

5. Distribute the newspapers, paper, glue, and scissors. When all groups have their materials, the race may begin. Let the students know how much time they have initially, and remind them periodically how much time is left.

6. Call time and collect sheets.

Materials
(for each team)

- newspaper
- Newspaper Scavenger Hunt (page 10)
- large sheets of paper
- glue sticks
- scissors

CHALLENGE

Ask students what other kinds of information could be included in a newspaper scavenger hunt. Assign students to create their own newspaper scavenger hunts to share with other students or classes.

Name _____ Date _____

NEWSPAPER SCAVENGER HUNT

- ☐ a letter to the editor
- ☐ a sportswriter's name
- ☐ ad for a pet dog
- ☐ the name of the president of the United States
- ☐ the flag
- ☐ an article about nature
- ☐ the name of your state's governor
- ☐ something that uses electricity
- ☐ the word *computer*
- ☐ a movie schedule
- ☐ a byline
- ☐ a masthead
- ☐ the name of your city or town

- ☐ names of three different countries
- ☐ a number larger than 1,000
- ☐ an article about education
- ☐ the name of your state
- ☐ a dateline
- ☐ a word in boldface
- ☐ an ad for a job working with people
- ☐ the expected high temperature for today
- ☐ a cutline
- ☐ a picture of a politician
- ☐ three words or pictures about transportation
- ☐ a picture of a sports star

Getting the Most Out of Teaching With Newspapers Scholastic Professional Books

NEWS WORD FLASH

In this cooperative game, teams select the word that fits the meaning.

What to Do

1. Make two sets of glossary cards, placing each glossary word on one index card.

2. Divide the class into two teams.

3. Pass one set of glossary cards to each team, so that each student has at least one word.

4. When teams are ready, hold up a newspaper and point to a part represented by one of the following vocabulary words: *banner, byline, classified ads, cutline, dateline, ear, editorial, feature, flag, gutter, hard news, headline, index, lead,* and *masthead.* (Feel free to add other terms to the card deck to create an appropriate challenge for your students.) Team members may collaborate before a student waves a word card to answer for the team.

5. To the first team that correctly identifies the newspaper part, give a letter in the word *NEWSPAPER.* For example, when you point to the newspaper name at the top of the newspaper, give a letter *N* to the first team to wave the *flag* word card.

6. Add a letter each time a team is first to choose the correct word. If there is a tie, both teams may gain a letter.

7. If you choose to create a full deck of 40 cards using all the newspaper terms, read definitions from the glossary or make up sentences for those terms to which you cannot point (e.g., *deadline*).

Materials

- 30 index cards (2 sets of 15)
- Newspaper Glossary (page 62), for each student
- newspaper

Tip:

Make transparencies for parts of the paper that are more difficult for students to see and identify.

DOUBLE MEANINGS

Many words used to describe newspaper editing and design work are familiar to students, but they take on very different meanings in the context of newspaper publishing. As they complete the picture puzzles on the Double Meanings reproducible, students will find how their understanding of familiar words matches the newspaper term definitions. This is an activity that's sure to surprise and amuse students, as well as teach newspaper lingo and expand their understanding of multiple definitions.

Flag

TODAY'S NEWS ⟩ Flag

What to Do

1. Review the directions on the reproducible.

2. Complete one or two examples with the class, matching the common definition suggested by the picture with the newspaper term definition from the glossary.

3. When students are finished, review the answers and discuss double meanings using the critical thinking questions that follow.

Materials
(for each student)
- Newspaper Glossary (page 62)
- Double Meanings (page 13)

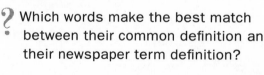

CRITICAL THINKING QUESTIONS

? In what ways are the newspaper meanings similar to the common definitions?

? Which words make the best match between their common definition and their newspaper term definition?

Answers to Double Meanings (page 13): 1. cover, 2. lead, 3. flag, 4. crop, 5. release, 6. scoop, 7. ear, 8. cut, 9. gutter, 10. jump (Definitions related to the newspaper are found in the glossary.)

DOUBLE MEANINGS

In newspaper lingo, words you use every day take on new meanings! Check your Newspaper Glossary to solve these picture puzzles: Match the picture to a newspaper term in the glossary. Then write meaning of the word that a newspaper publisher would use.

WORD	NEWSPAPER MEANING	WORD	NEWSPAPER MEANING

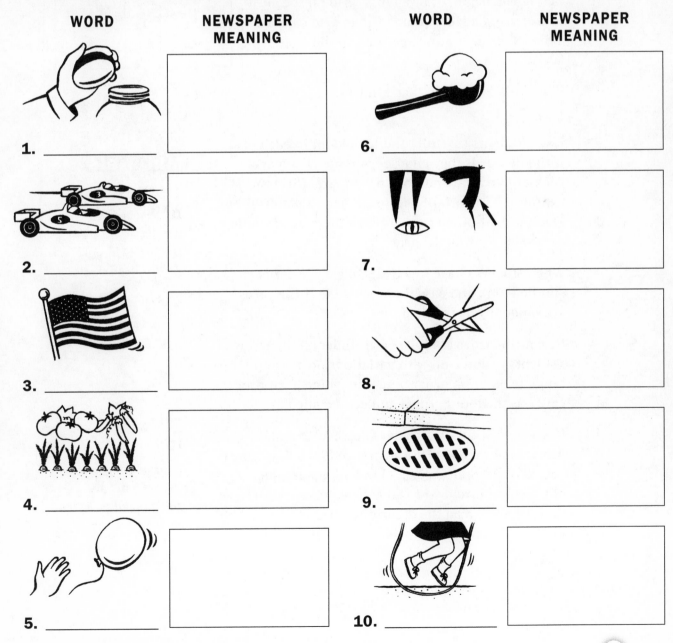

1. _____

2. _____

3. _____

4. _____

5. _____

6. _____

7. _____

8. _____

9. _____

10. _____

MEDIA LINGO BINGO

While creating a game board and playing Media Lingo Bingo, students review newspaper terms in a fun and easy way. The game can be adapted to help students review specialized terms used by producers of other media such as TV, radio, and Internet.

M	**E**	**D**	**I**	**A**
gutter	ear	headline	cover	break
dummy	byline	layout	columnist	index
scoop	correspondent	Free Space	cut	editorial
feature	release	flag	hard news	filler
classified ads	dateline	wire service	jump	banner

Getting the Most Out of Teaching With Newspapers Scholastic Professional Books 15

What to Do

1. Before you begin, draw a bingo grid on the board, using a Media Lingo Bingo grid card as a model, or have a transparency of the page available.

2. Pass out materials to each student.

3. Have students carefully and legibly fill in each grid with any words they choose from the Newspaper Glossary, writing one word per square. (Stress that neatness is important because other students will be reading their bingo cards.) Show them an example or two on your model grid.

4. When students have finished, collect the cards, shuffle them, and pass them out so that the cards are randomly distributed.

5. Review the rules of bingo with students. Encourage students to come up with variations on scoring for bingo (e.g., four-corner bingo, in which a winning card has the four corners and center filled).

6. Use a copy of the Newspaper Glossary, to call out the definition or using a clue sentence for each word you randomly select (e.g., "I'm looking at a picture of a tropical bird next to an article on saving Brazil's rain forests. I read the description written below the picture. What's that called in newspaper lingo?" *Cutline)*

Materials
(for each student)
- ☐ Media Lingo Bingo grid card (page 15)
- ☐ Newspaper Glossary (page 62)
- ☐ at least 15 beans or other markers

Tip:
To make the game more challenging, have students put away their definitions during play.

MEDIA LINGO BINGO

M E D I A

		Free Space		

PART TWO

USING THE NEWSPAPER AS A LEARNING TOOL

Quick Tips: *Enhancing lessons with newspapers*

CURRENT EVENTS LEARNING LOGS

▨ In their learning logs, students write to learn, reflect, and respond to topics introduced in the newspaper. Learning logs can be a notebook or simply papers stapled into a folder. Many of the activities in this section provide writing ideas for learning logs. By selecting a specific item for each entry (e.g., grammar, content, creativity, and spelling), you can make an assessment of the individual entries.

NEWSPAPER SLEUTHS

▨ Satisfy students' urge to help by recruiting those who finish assignments early to collect articles and other interesting parts of the newspaper for reading and other upcoming activities or theme units. They can clip, sort, arrange, and file articles, maps, comics, charts, graphs, political cartoons, weather maps, and photographs to use for future lessons.

▨ Assign a student or group of helpers one specific item to look for at a time. As students read and talk about what is in the paper, they will be making note of interesting current events, information from many areas, and surprising facts, and will become familiar with the layout of the newspaper.

BULLETIN BOARDS WITH THE FULL SCOOP

▨ Newspaper-related bulletin boards give wandering eyes a place to rest and learn. Relating articles and pictures to a theme your class has studied makes the display more interesting.

▨ Whenever possible, make a bulletin board interactive, a place where students can add their own ideas (attach new articles or other items) or actively learn from the information. Near the bulletin board, place a folder or basket that contains fun and challenging questions, puzzles, searches, questionnaires, or activity ideas for students to complete in their spare time. These high-interest activities might include a blank interview sheet ready for completion, a daily question about a "hot" current event, and a science concept in the news that might be accessed through an on-line paper and posted on the bulletin board.

Newspaper activities enrich word skill instruction by using real examples and news events in context, rather than feeding students the unrelated sentences found in skills books and on worksheets.

ACRONYMS AND ABBREVIATIONS

Students become familiar with and learn commonly used acronyms and abbreviations—word knowledge that will help them read the newspaper with greater fluency.

NYFD
BOE   AP
Sen. Fri.
       Yr. NHL
       U.N.

What to Do

1. Students may notice, or you might point out, that one of the differences between the way copy (the text on a page) is set in books and the way it is set in newspapers is that newspapers use a large number of acronyms and abbreviations.

2. Ask students why they think acronyms or abbreviations are used so frequently in newspapers. (Answers should address issues of space and repetition.)

3. Explain to students that becoming familiar with standard acronyms and abbreviations will help them read the paper more effectively.

4. Start a class chart to keep track of common acronyms and abbreviations and define what each stands for. Draw a simple three-column table and begin the table with a few examples.

Acronym	Abbreviation	Stands For
	TV	television
D.A.R.E.		Drug Abuse Resistance Education
	Dr.	doctor
	NFL	National Football League

5. Keep the chart handy in the room for students to add to as they read the paper.

Materials

(for each team)
- chart paper
- newspaper advertisements

CHALLENGE

- When the chart is filled with 20 or more terms, challenge students to write a silly story using as many acronyms and abbreviations as possible.

- Have students create their own classroom set of acronyms that are understandable and applicable only to them!

HEADLINE SCRAMBLE

Students manipulate sentence structure and adjust meaning.

What to Do

1 Cut out from the paper headlines that are five words or longer.

2 Cut apart each headline word by word and place the separated words in envelopes, numbering each envelope. (Number the first envelope *1*. Then write *1* on the back of each word in that envelope. Number envelope 2 and headline 2 in the same way, and so on.) Keep as a reference a photocopy or list of all the original headlines you've used for this activity.

3 Distribute envelopes to individual students or pairs. Challenge students to find as many ways as possible to arrange each set of words into a headline that makes sense. They should choose the order they think sounds best and record their answers on index cards. Make sure students write the number of the envelope on their index card to make checking answers easy.

4 Compare their new headlines to the original ones in the newspaper. Discuss how students' headlines are similar to or different from the original headlines. Let students explore how different placement of words creates different emphasis (e.g., "Dancers Wait for Jazz Choreographers" could be "Choreographers Wait for Jazz Dancers"). Students may also experiment with punctuation ("Choreographers: 'Wait for Jazz, Dancers!'")

Materials

- ☒ 15 or more headlines, cut out
- ☒ envelopes
- ☒ index cards

SALES TALK

Students learn why the use of particular words helps to sell a product. They will learn the concept of writing to a specific audience.

What to Do

1. Students look for words and slogans advertisers use to help sell their products. Start your discussion by asking why words like *bargain*, *save*, *quality*, *amazing*, and *value* are used to grab the reader's attention.

2. Ask students to evaluate how other words and slogans grab the reader's attention and make the product sound appealing.

3. Have them each select the ad that is most appealing to them and the ad they think would be most appealing to the adults in their families. Use the critical thinking questions that follow as a discussion guide or as written response prompts for learning logs.

Materials

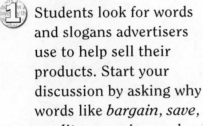

☐ ads from newspapers (enough so that each student has 2 or 3)

CRITICAL THINKING QUESTIONS

? Which words get you interested in the product? Which words would get the attention of the adults in your family?

? Choose the three most powerful advertising words in the ads. Why do you think these words are important? How do slogans help sell products?

EXTENSION

Design an Ad

Encourage students to write their own ads for a product they create. On the board, create a list of products young people use (sneakers, hair products, snacks, and so on). Have students create their own words that describe a particular product as popular or fun to use. Alternatively, you can challenge students to use ideas from the social studies or science curriculum to design and write an ad for a new product that they think would appeal to their peers. For example, during a unit on electricity, a student might "invent" an electrical appliance for doing a chore they don't enjoy, or a new, healthy snack food during a nutrition unit. You can use these ads when you make a class paper. (See Part Three.)

WHAT'S THE BIG IDEA?

Students practice identifying the main idea of an article by writing their own headlines. Note that finding the main idea in newspaper articles is often easier than finding it in a passage or story because newspaper articles are written to provide concise information and usually address one topic in a very focused way. After having practiced finding main ideas in newspaper articles, students may develop a clearer idea about what to look for in other writing.

Headline: Oil Spill Covers Miles of Shoreline

What to Do

1 Read and review with the class an article without its headline. Ask students to list facts from the article. Record their responses on the board and have the class narrow down the key information by crossing out details and less important facts.

2 From this work, ask students to agree on a main idea statement—"the big idea" of the article. (It may help students to make a summary with the 5 W's, which they can usually find in the lead paragraph.)

3 Using their main idea statement, have each student write his or her own headline that succinctly tells the main idea of the article in 5 to 7 words. Let students share their headlines with the class, and encourage them to compare their headlines and talk about the differences. Can the class come up with an even shorter (3 to 5 words) headline that everyone agrees on?

4 Finally, display the orginal headline and have students determine which headline expresses the main idea best, the class's version or the newspaper's.

5 Locate other articles of interest to students and repeat the activity either as a class, with students in pairs, or for independent practice.

Materials

- article with headline removed, photo-copied to create a class set and available as a transparency
- additional newspaper articles with headlines removed (save the headlines for the Headlines to Sentences activity, page 21)

20

HEADLINES TO SENTENCES

Headlines are usually written as sentence fragments and make great tools for teaching the concepts of complete sentences and elaboration.

What to Do

1. Pass out three headlines to each student or pair.

2. Ask students to decide if the headlines are complete sentences.

3. Have a few students share reasons for their decisions. Ask students to think about what the headlines need to become complete sentences. Students may notice common practices such as the elimination of articles—*a, an, the* ("Dog Saves Child")—and even verbs ("Senator: No New Taxes!") to save space.

4. Have students change one of their headlines into a sentence. They can paste or copy the fragment (headline) onto the butcher paper and write their complete sentence below it. (This creates a class record of students' work on sentence structure.)

5. On their own, students glue their other two headlines to a piece of paper and rewrite them as complete sentences below.

6. Have students review their work in pairs, or collect and assess the work.

Dog Saves Child!

A courageous golden retriever pulls a drowning three-year-old from a backyard pool.

Materials

(for each student or pair)

☐ 3 newspaper headlines
☐ lined paper
☐ glue sticks
☐ butcher paper (should accommodate 12–15 headline pairs)

CHALLENGE

Distribute articles with fragment headlines attached. Have students create complete, well-elaborated sentences by using details from the articles to add information and interest.

CONVERSATION STARTERS

Using cartoons as springboards, students practice writing dialogue between characters, applying appropriate punctuation and paragraphing skills.

What to Do

1 Pass out the comic strips to students.

2 Ask students how they know that the characters are speaking. Explain how quotation marks are used to highlight dialogue in other types of writing. (Students should recognize that comic-strip dialogue is represented by speech balloons. In stories, authors use quotation marks to indicate dialogue.)

3 Ask students to write their comic strips using quotation marks and other punctuation correctly. If students are unfamiliar with punctuating dialogue, you might start by having them simply list the lines of dialogue, skipping down to a new line and indenting every time a different character speaks. They may place quotation marks around the complete words of each speaker. Remind students that they can indicate who is talking by adding tag lines (*he said* or *she screamed*). Students with more writing experience may vary their placement of the tag lines (at beginning, end, or middle of the quotation) and add descriptions of the setting and action. To provide guidance, model new elements on the board or overhead projector.

4 As an additional exercise, conduct a mini-lesson on how to use the thesaurus. Gather some great synonyms for the word *said* and have students experiment using these synonyms in their tag lines.

Materials

☒ comic strips that include dialogue bubbles, 1 strip, or a copy of the same strip, for each student

SOCIAL STUDIES ACTIVITIES

Newspapers provide opportunities for students to learn about their world in a meaningful way, through current events in international, national, and local events.

WHERE IN THE WORLD?

In this activity, students locate on a world map countries featured in current events and news articles.

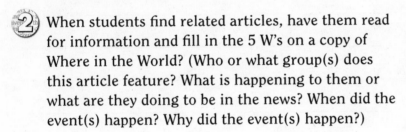

What to Do

1. Have students scan newspapers to find articles about other countries. You might assign or let students choose a focus country.

2. When students find related articles, have them read for information and fill in the 5 W's on a copy of Where in the World? (Who or what group(s) does this article feature? What is happening to them or what are they doing to be in the news? When did the event(s) happen? Why did the event(s) happen?)

3. Have students cut out the articles and post them around a large world map.

4. String colored yarn between articles and the appropriate locations on the map.

Materials

- large world map fastened to a bulletin board (should be within students' reach)
  (for each team)
- Globe or world map
- yarn
- newspapers
- scissors
- Where in the World? (page 24), 1 for each student

EXTENSION

Worldwide Scavenger Hunt

1. After students have found 10 or more different locations, devise a world geography scavenger hunt. Divide students into groups of three. Give each group a globe (you may need to borrow globes from other classrooms for this activity) and a sheet of questions based on the articles displayed around the world map. For instance, ask: *On what island did a volcano erupt recently? What ocean surrounds this island?* Design questions so that students must refer to both the displayed articles and their globes.

2. Have students create their own questions about these featured locations and write the questions on index cards. Set up the question cards as a center activity near the bulletin board so that students can work in front of the map to find answers. Or incorporate student questions into a quiz or Jeopardy-style geography game.

Name _____   Date _____

WHERE IN THE WORLD?

Use this page to help you take notes on a country or countries in the news!
As you read, ask yourself, *Who or what people or groups does this article
feature? What is happening to them or what are they doing to be
in the news? When and where did the event happen? Why did the event
happen?*

1 Headline: _____

country: _____   continent: _____

who: _____

what: _____

when/where: _____

why: _____

2 Headline: _____

country: _____   continent: _____

who: _____

what: _____

when/where: _____

why: _____

3 Headline: _____

country: _____   continent: _____

who: _____

what: _____

when/where: _____

why: _____

Getting the Most Out of Teaching With Newspapers Scholastic Professional Books

THE STATE YOU'RE IN

Students learn about important subjects in regional news and locate on a state map the city or town in focus.

What to Do

1. Divide students into groups of three. Have each group collect 12 articles about their state.

2. Have groups read their set of articles and discuss how to distinguish each article by subtopic. They should agree on four to six categories (e.g., sports, politics, government, family, and so forth) based on the subtopics they've generated.

3. Let each group make a chart on a piece of butcher paper, writing their category names in large squares and then gluing the articles in the appropriate category.

4. Have students find the location featured in each article. They should place a colored dot sticker next to the city or town name in the article and the same colored dot on the state wall map.

Materials

- state wall map (for each group)
- large pieces of butcher paper
- scissors
- markers
- newspapers
- glue sticks
- removable colored dot stickers

Current Events in California

sports	medicine	environment
government	famous people	health

FIFTY FINDERS

Students love a contest! In this geography activity, teams find articles about as many U.S. states as possible, allowing them the opportunity to learn a great deal about the geography, culture, and politics of different regions. Make this an ongoing project (about one to three weeks), which students can do either when they've finished other work or for a designated time during the day.

What to Do

1. Explain that the class is going to have a contest to see which teams can locate articles about the most states.

2. Encourage the class to gather papers from friends or family in other states. You may want to obtain some national publications such as *USA Today* or seek out on-line publications to provide better coverage of regions not in your area.

3. Set the time frame and expectations for collecting articles.

4. As students find articles, they should cut them out, staple them to notebook paper, and number them. Distribute copies of the Fifty Finders U.S. Map.

5. Ask students to highlight the name of the state or states found in each article, and then write the number of the article on the corresponding state on the map. The Fifty Finders reproducible also asks them to color in the featured state and label on the map a city name or geographic feature mentioned in the article. Each group should keep their articles clipped together with their map.

6. Keep a running tally sheet posted to show how many states each group has found.

Materials

- Fifty Finders U.S. Map (page 27), 1 copy for each student
- white paper
- newspapers
- glue sticks
- scissors

EXTENSION

Most-Mentioned State Graph

Have students create a bar graph that shows how many articles they have found about each state or region. Initiate a class discussion about why certain states are in the news so much at this time.

FIFTY FINDERS U.S. MAP

Each time you find and article about one of the 50 states, color that state on the map below. List one geographic feature or city mentioned in the article and use a map of that state to locate the place. Then label the place on this map.

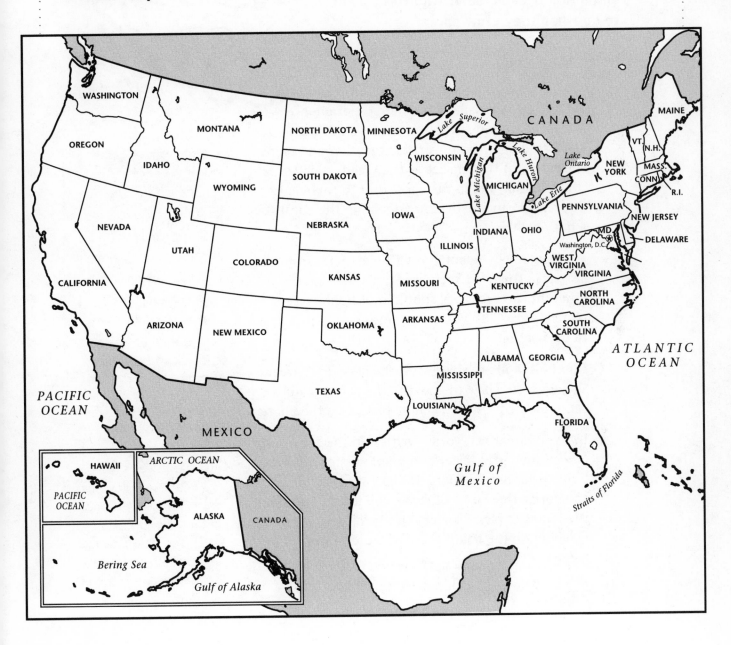

JOBS IN THE NEWS BINGO

Career education begins with awareness of the variety of jobs that keep our communities functioning. As students scramble to discover what occupations are in the news, they learn the importance of various occupations and start to think about what they want to be when they grow up.

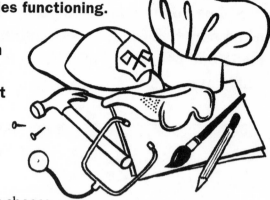

What to Do

1. From the front page of the newspaper choose an article that involves one or more occupations. Have students read the article together and name the career(s) they notice as they read. Help students understand these in the context of the article (e.g., a Supreme Court justice mentioned in the context of a national trial).

2. Working independently or with partners, students search in the front section of a newspaper for 10 different careers. They should highlight career names, as well as words and phrases that give clues to occupations.

3. Invite students to share with the class the careers they located. Have them write the career names on sentence strips, which can be tacked on the board.

4. List the career categories written in the Jobs in the News Bingo grid (or draw a giant version of this bingo grid) on the board. Call on students to categorize the careers they've collected by sticking their slips of paper under the appropriate job category on the board (e.g., NFL coach under "Sports"). Students are now ready to locate and categorize careers when playing Jobs in the News Bingo.

Materials
(for each student)
- newspapers
- highlighters
- sentence strips
- markers
- scissors
- glue sticks
- Jobs-in-the-News Bingo (page 30)

28

Directions for Jobs in the News Bingo

1. Pass out newspapers and a copy of Jobs in the News Bingo to each student or group. (This game works best when students play in pairs or groups of three.)

2. Direct students to cut out phrases or words that describe careers and glue them in the correct category boxes. Remind students that some jobs may fall under two different career categories and have them choose the category best represented by the article.

3. Create a level of challenge that is appropriate for your students: Winners might need to fill in all the boxes or only the traditional five in a row.

Name _Alix_   Date _2-12_

JOBS IN THE NEWS BINGO

Search for an example of one job title or description from each category below as you read the newspaper. List or paste the clipping in the right box. Can you fill in five in a row? How about the whole board?

Environment	Legal	Education
Human Services West Virginia:	Technical President of TechFlo (two technologies)	Military peacekeepers
Science	Sports	Manufacturing
Arts and Entertainment lead actor	Political	Agricultural
Media	Construction	Business

30   Getting the Most Out of Teaching With Newspapers Scholastic Professional Books

CRITICAL THINKING QUESTIONS

? What jobs fit under more than one heading?

? Which career categories were easiest to find? Which were hardest? Why do you think there is less information about these?

? What jobs do you think are easiest to find? Why?

? How do you think the grid would look if you played this game with a newspaper that was 50 years old?

EXTENSION

Careers Then

Have students find a newspaper from 40, 50, or 60 years ago and discover the careers listed there and compare them to present-day occupations. Most local newspapers have Web sites on the Internet. You can call your local paper to find out how to locate old copies of newspapers. A good Web site for retrieving archived U.S. newspaper publications is www.newspaperlinks.com.

Name _____ Date _____

JOBS IN THE NEWS BINGO

Search for an example of one job title or description from each category below as you read the newspaper. List or paste the clipping in the right box. Can you fill in five in a row? How about the whole board?

Environment	Legal	Education
Human Services	**Technical**	**Military**
Science	**Sports**	**Manufacturing**
Arts and Entertainment	**Political**	**Agricultural**
Media	**Construction**	**Business**

Getting the Most Out of Teaching With Newspapers Scholastic Professional Books

MY KIND OF JOB

Students use the classified ads as a stimulus for researching and discovering qualifications for a job that interests them.

WANTED:

Design layout editor for small classroom newspaper. Must be familiar with setting articles, pictures, and captions.

What to Do

1. Encourage students to search through the classified ads to locate several different jobs they might like to have. Let students share their job ideas with a partner or small group to generate discussion about the pros and cons of the jobs they've identified.

2. Ask each student to select the most appealing job from his or her collected ads. (Have them consider the elements of the job that most appeal to them—type of work, sedentary/mobile, indoor/outdoor, salary, and so forth.)

3. Using the chosen ad, students can respond to any of the following questions in their learning logs or journals, or on a paper to be handed in or shared. (Note that some of these questions require them to ask for input from family members or do further research on the Internet.)

Materials

(for each student)
- ☐ learning log, journal, or lined paper
- ☐ classified ad section
- ☐ Classified Ads Search (pages 32–33)

1. Pretend you are the employer who wrote this ad. Write a list of five important questions you would ask someone wanting to work for you.

2. Form a list of qualifications needed to apply for this job.

3. Ask an adult (parent, teacher, relative) to tell you everything he or she knows about this type of work and take notes.

4. Use the Internet to search for information about the occupation that you chose. Record new information.

5. Write why you would want this job. What skills do you have already that would help you in this line of work?

6. Describe what you think your first day of work would be like.

4. Distribute copies of the Classified Ads Search to help students understand how to read the classified section critically and analyze information presented there. Encourage students to take home their page and a section of the classifieds. They can discuss and compare with the adults in their families types of jobs available now and those available years or even decades ago. Use the reproducible as a discussion guide when students have finished.

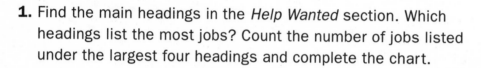

Name _____ Date _____

CLASSIFIED ADS SEARCH

Look in the *Help Wanted* section of the classified ads to answer these questions.

1. Find the main headings in the *Help Wanted* section. Which headings list the most jobs? Count the number of jobs listed under the largest four headings and complete the chart.

	Heading	Number of Listings
1	_____	_____
2	_____	_____
3	_____	_____
4	_____	_____

2. Look under the heading that lists the largest number of jobs. How many of these jobs require training or education past high school? _____

3. What do you notice about the difference in salaries between jobs that require more training or education and those that require less or none?

_____

_____

4. What skills, no matter what the job, are all employers looking for in people they hire?

_____

_____

_____

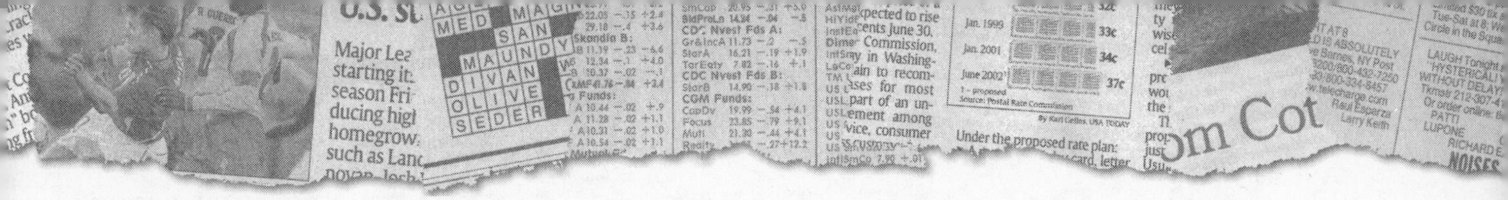

Name _____ Date _____

5. Choose what you think are the three best jobs in the classified section. Explain why you think these would be good jobs to have.

job: _____ reason: _____

_____

job: _____ reason: _____

_____

job: _____ reason: _____

_____

6. How do you think the job market has changed since your parents were your age?

_____

_____

_____

_____

7. Ask the adults in your family how they think the job market has changed since they were your age. Record their answers to share with the class.

_____

_____

_____

_____

_____

_____

HANDS OF THE GOVERNMENT BULLETIN BOARD

Newspaper articles related to the U.S. federal government help students find out how the different branches of the government have an impact on issues in the news.

NOTE: *Before you begin this activity, make sure students are familiar with the three branches of government and the different functions they serve.*

What to Do

1 Give the bulletin board a colorful background and the title "Hands of the Government." Make a sign for each branch of the government. Use the colors of the flag to distinguish the signs (red for legislative, white for judicial, blue for executive). Post the signs on a cutout tree with branches, or simply set them in three columns with space below for students to attach the hand cutouts.

> Executive Branch   Legislative Branch   Judicial Branch

2 Working in groups or individually, students should collect 3–6 articles that mention the federal government. Have them highlight the part of the article that mentions the branch of the government that is involved in the issue. Students may refer to any resource that lists the branches of the government (copy and enlarge the diagram on page 35) for help identifying key terms and offices that refer to each branch. You may want to collect and review a few articles as a class to review the three branches of government.

3 Have students read their own articles and identify which branch of the government is mentioned. On a construction paper hand cutout that matches the appropriate government branch color, students should write the newspaper title, article title, page number, and date of publication, and give short answers to the 5 W's: Who? What? When? Where? Why? To check responses, have students hand in their articles.

Materials

(for each student, pair, or group)

☐ newspapers
☐ red, white, and blue construction paper "hand" cutouts (3–6)
☐ scissors
☐ markers
☐ highlighters
☐ references that list the offices under each branch of government

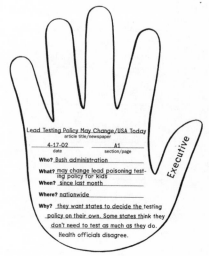

Lead Testing Policy May Change/USA Today
article title/newspaper

4-17-02   A1
date   section/page

Who? Bush administration

What? may change lead poisoning testing policy for kids

When? since last month

Where? nationwide

Why? they want states to decide the testing
policy on their own. Some states think they
don't need to test as much as they do.
Health officials disagree.

Executive

4 Invite students to place the completed paper hands underneath the appropriate branch of government. Allow students to explain to the class why they are placing a summary under a particular heading.

5 As a class, discuss why certain branches and departments might have more "hands" in the news.

UNITED STATES GOVERNMENT

Executive Branch	Legislative Branch	Judicial Branch
White House	**House of Representatives**	**Supreme Court**
President	**Senate**	
Vice President		

Cabinet Departments

Agriculture	Housing	Labor
CIA	Health and	State
Commerce	Human Services	Transportation
Defense	Interior	Treasury
Education	Justice (Attorney	Veterans Affairs
Energy	General, FBI)	

Name _____ Date _____

HANDS OF THE GOVERNMENT
TEMPLATE

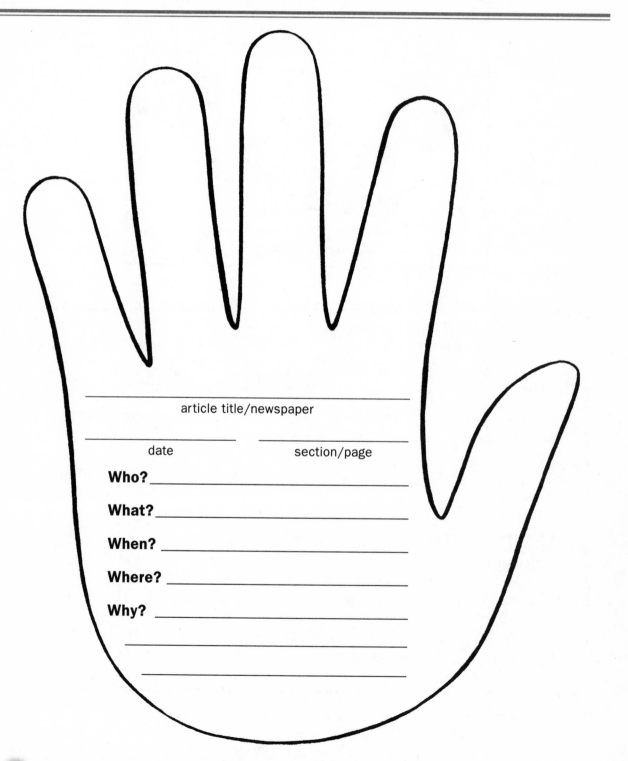

_____
article title/newspaper

_____   _____
date   section/page

Who? _____

What? _____

When? _____

Where? _____

Why? _____

_____

_____

GLOBAL GOVERNMENTS

While reading articles about different countries, students will learn about the various forms of world government.

	Global Governments			
Continent	Country	Capital	Leader	Type of Government
Asia	India	New Delhi	Vajpayee	federal republic

What to Do

1. Send students on a search for different countries mentioned in the newspaper. Have each student find three articles about three different countries.

2. Discuss the various forms of government that exist in the world. Pick those you feel are most critical for students to learn at this level, such as democracy, monarchy, oligarchy, and dictatorship.

3. As they collect articles, have students identify the focus countries and read reference materials or use the Internet to find more information about each country's form of government.

4. Make a large chart on which students can list the countries they have learned about. The chart may be organized by continent and have columns in which to record the country's capital, leader, and form of government (other categories might include population and major religions). Number the countries on the chart.

5. Invite each student to mark on the world map the location of one of the countries he or she studied, using a numbered, colored circle sticker that corresponds to the country on the chart. (More advanced students may want to classify the different government types by sticker color.) Hang the chart next to the map; now the class has a visual reference for learning about types of governments around the world.

6. Discuss the sizes of countries and how the type of government influences that country's way of life and impact on the world.

Materials

- wall-sized world map
- removable circle stickers
- chart paper or butcher paper

WEB LINK: The CIA's World Fact Book
http://www.odci.gov/cia/publications/factbook/index.html
provides easy-to-navigate facts about each country along with map resources.

RULES TO LIVE BY

By reading articles about U.S. legal issues, students will learn about the Bill of Rights.

Congress of the United States

THE ———
RESOLVED ———
ARTICLES ———

What to Do

1. Provide students with some background on the Bill of Rights and discuss its important place in the constitution and U.S. history (see Web Links for on-line resources). Explain that the Bill of Rights is only the first ten amendments to the Constitution and that 17 more have been added since 1791 for a total of 27 amendments.

2. Pass out copies of the Bill of Rights—The Original Ten reproducible and review with students the original ten amendments, which are explained in simple terms. Ask for examples of how people's rights have been or might be protected by these amendments.

3. In groups, have students search for 2–5 articles that bring up legal problems that can be related to any of these amendments.

4. Write each of the ten amendments of the Bill of Rights on a large piece of butcher paper and post it on the wall or a bulletin board where students can reach it easily. Have students glue or tack their articles under the appropriate amendment heading and write on an index card a short explanation of how the article relates to the amendment.

Materials

- ✗ Bill of Rights— The Original Ten (page 39), 1 copy for each student
- ✗ newspapers
- ✗ large sheets of butcher paper
- ✗ glue sticks
- ✗ scissors
- ✗ index cards

CRITICAL THINKING QUESTIONS

? How have human rights been protected because of the Bill of Rights?

? Which amendments are still debated today? (Students may use the information they've gathered from their articles and from other sources listed in the Web Links section.)

? Did any amendment surprise you? (Can students relate how Amendment III resulted from the British occupation before and during the American Revolution?)

? Have students research one of the 17 later amendments. In a paragraph in their learning logs, journals, or notebooks, have students explain the amendment and why they think it is important to American life today.

WEB LINKS: There are many wonderful resources on the Internet to help teachers teach about the Constitution and Bill of Rights.

Original Scanned Documents
http://www.law.emory.edu/FEDERAL/conpict.html

The Bill of Rights: A Brief History
(American Civil Liberties Union)
http://www.aclu.org/library/pbp9.html

The Constitution by Net
http://Constitution.by.net

The Federalist Archive
http://federalist.freeservers.com

EXTENSION

Classroom Bill of Rights

Ask students to consider what rights learners and teachers should have in a classroom. Have groups of four or five students work together to come up with a bill of rights for the classroom. Review each group's rules and have students vote on the five rules they think are the most important to post in the room. Then live by those rules for a week. Discuss how the rules worked and if they should be changed, or amended. Make amendments as needed and relate what you've done to the way our government may change or add to laws. Make the connection with why government rules sometimes need to be altered.

Name _____ Date _____

BILL OF RIGHTS—
THE ORIGINAL TEN

The Bill of Rights is a set of ten amendments that were added to the Constitution in 1791 to protect the rights of the United States citizens. The following is a summary of the original amendments. Since this time, 17 more have been added to the Constitution. Search the newspaper to find articles that relate to these original ten amendments.

Amendment I Congress may not make rules to limit freedom of religion, freedom of the press, freedom of speech, or the right of people to come together in a peaceful way.

Amendment II Citizens (except for children and convicted criminals) have the right to keep and bear arms.

Amendment III During peacetime, the government cannot force citizens to house soldiers in their homes.

Amendment IV People and their personal property may not be searched unreasonably.

Amendment V People accused of a crime may not be forced to give evidence against themselves or have their lives, freedom, or property taken from them unfairly.

Amendment VI People accused of crimes have the right to a speedy trial.

Amendment VII In most noncriminal cases, there must be a right to a jury trial.

Amendment VIII Punishment must not be cruel and unusual. A court decides what *cruel and unusual* means.

Amendments IX/X If the Constitution does not give a certain right to the U.S. government, but also does not forbid a state government to have that right, then the states and the people have it.

MATH AND SCIENCE ACTIVITIES

From advertisements to stock quotes and breaking news on the latest discoveries about Pluto, the newspaper provides many ready-to-go resources for math and science activities.

NEWSWORTHY NUMBERS

Students discover how numbers help us get a clearer picture of the news.

$2K   100%

¼   .00391

20°F   562 lbs.

What to Do

1 Give students 10 minutes to search the front page to find and highlight as many different types of numbers as they can. (This search should generate a long list, from page number references to temperature readings.) As a class, list and review the ways numbers are used.

2 Ask students how these articles would read without numbers. Have them try reading their articles to a partner, replacing numbers with general words like *big*, *a few*, *lots*, *tall*, *fast*, and *many*. What questions do those generalizations leave them with? Ask students how specific number facts can help people better understand the news.

3 Challenge students to think analytically and drive home this point. Distribute the article in which you have deleted specific numbers and replaced them with general terms. Have students make reasonable guesses and fill in the crossed-out spaces with specific numbers. Then pass out the original and encourage them to compare their filled-in version.

Materials
(for each student)

- newspapers
- highlighters
- newspaper article containing numerical data (dates, times, earnings, sports statistics, and so forth). A short sports article or any report rich in numbers and quantities of things kids relate to (toys, movies, and so forth) would work well.
- copy of the above article with all the numbers blacked out and replaced with general value terms

SALARY SLEUTHS

Students compute the salaries they might earn in their ideal careers and find out what it takes to "make it" in today's world. This activity can be used in tandem with the career activities on pages 28 and 31.

What to Do

1. Have a class discussion about students' future career ideas. Let them estimate what they think a person would earn during a year doing this job.

2. Pass out classified advertisements. Have students find several listings for the job they want.

3. Students then cut out the listings and paste them into their learning logs, journals, or notebooks.

4. Present a short lesson on how to figure out earnings for a month, a week, and a day using the salaries quoted by the ads. Depending on how the jobs are advertised, you may need to model how to multiply hourly wages to figure out yearly wages or divide the yearly wage into monthly or weekly earnings.

5. Let students compute the hourly, daily, weekly, and yearly earnings for the job they have chosen. More advanced students can do this for several ads and compare their potential incomes from each.

Materials
(for each student)
- ☒ classified section
- ☒ scissors
- ☒ glue stick
- ☒ learning log, journal, or notebook

EXTENSION

Be the Breadwinner
Have students look for apartment rentals in the classifieds and choose an apartment with the space, features, and location that they want. Have them ask their parents how much they spend on utilities, food, gas, and so forth, for a month. Using these figures, have students estimate how much it would cost for them to feed, clothe, and shelter themselves (and their families) each month. Can they do it with the salary for the jobs they have chosen? If not, what might they change?

CHARTS AND GRAPHS IN THE NEWS

Students will understand the use of graphs and charts in the newspaper and learn to interpret them.

What to Do

 Have students glue the charts or graphs from the newspaper into their learning logs, journals, or notebooks.

 Using the overhead projector, discuss each graph or chart with the class. Then ask students to write a sentence or two below each graphic, interpreting what facts it illustrates. Encourage students to look for patterns in the data, and for the highest and lowest numbers. Ask students to explain how they think the data will change over time, or how the data make a difference to readers.

Materials

- ☒ copies of 3-5 charts and graphs from the newspaper, 1 set for each student
- ☒ transparency of each chart or graph
- ☒ glue sticks
- ☒ learning logs, journals, or notebooks

STOCK MARKET MATH

While using math skills to interpret stock market quotes, students learn how the stock market works.

What to Do

1 Guide students through the information and examples provided by The Stock Market News reproducible to show them how to read stock market quotes. Answer the first set of questions on page 45 together (see answers below). Students should notice that the decimals translate easily into dollars.

2 Encourage students to use the business section to find information about stocks from companies they recognize. Compare and ask questions about daily stock quotes from these companies.

3 Have students follow a stock of their choice to learn how to keep track of the ups and downs of the stock market.

Materials

- ☒ newspaper business section, 1 section for each student or pair
- ☒ The Stock Market News (page 45), 1 copy for each student

Answers

page 45	page 46
1. $60	1. TOY
2. $36.50	2. Happy Toy
3. Yum Cakes	3. Toyware ($10.23)
4. YCake	4. Toyware ($21.00)
5. $2.40	5. Toyware ($24.60)
6. $43.20	6. $21.50
7. $38.70	7. $23.00
8. $40.80	8. Toyware by 1.50
9. +$1.30; increase	9. Happy Toy
	10. Toyware

WEB LINKS: Money and investment education sites

The New York Stock Exchange
http://www.nyse.com

A. G. Edwards' Big Money Adventure
http://agedwards.com/public/bma/frontpage.fcgi

Online Math Applications
http://tqjunior.thinkquest.org/4116/
Includes a stock market game with authentic Wall Street data.

Name _____ Date _____

THE STOCK MARKET NEWS

Newspapers provide important information that helps investors decide which companies' stocks they want to buy. The chart below is similar to the one you'll find in the business section of a major newspaper. The parts are numbered and explained below. Use this information to help you understand how to read the stock quotes and answer the questions below.

SHARE: One of the equal parts into which a company's ownership is divided. When you buy a share of a company's stock, you become an owner.

DIVIDEND: The amount per share a company distributes to its stockholders.

1	2	3	4	5	6	7	8	9
52 Wk Hi	52 Wk Lo	Stock	Sym	Dividend	Hi	Lo	Close	Change
60	36.5	Yum Cakes	YCake	2.4	43.2	38.7	40.8	+1.3

1. The highest price paid for a share in the past 52 weeks (*52 Wk Hi*) $60

2. The lowest price paid for a share in the past 52 weeks (*52 Wk Lo*) _____

3. The name of the company (*Stock*) _____

4. The symbol (abbreviation) used to represent the company (*Sym*) _____

5. The points, or dollars, per share the company pays (*Dividend*) _____

6. The highest price per share for that day (*Hi*) _____

7. The lowest price per share for that day (*Lo*) _____

8. The price of a share at the end of the day (*Close*) _____

9. The amount of change from the closing of the day before (*Change*) _____
A **+** means the value is higher than the day before and a **–** means the value is lower. Did the value increase or decrease? _____

Name _____ Date _____

TOY COMPANY STOCK QUOTES
Use the following made-up stock quotes for Toyware and Happy Toy
to answer the questions below.

52 Wk Hi	52 Wk Lo	Stock	Sym	Dividend	Hi	Lo	Close	Change
26.75	10.23	Toyware	TOY	3.0	24.6	20.2	21	-2.0

52 Wk Hi	52 Wk Lo	Stock	Sym	Dividend	Hi	Lo	Close	Change
28.62	10.32	Happy Toy	HAP	2.4	22.3	18.8	22	+.5

1. What is the symbol for Toyware? _____

2. Which toy company had the higher share price during the past 52 weeks? _____

3. Which stock could have been bought for the cheaper price during the past year? _____

4. Which company ended lower for the day? _____

5. Which stock had the higher price during the day? _____

6. What was the closing price of Happy Toy stock yesterday? _____

7. What was the closing price of Toyware stock yesterday? _____

8. Which stock closed higher yesterday and by how many points? _____

9. Which stock closed closer to its highest price of the day? _____

10. Which company pays the higher dividend? _____

COST CUTTERS

Students learn to be savvy shoppers when they compare ads for their favorite products.

What to Do

1. Model how to find the cost per unit of items sold at discount and in different quantities. Here are some examples you can use:

   SuperInk pens: 4 for $1.20. The price of one pen = $0.30 ($1.20 ÷ 4).

   Yummy-O Gum is on sale at 25% off its regular price of $1.00 = $0.75. If there are five pieces in a pack, each piece costs $0.15 ($0.75 ÷ 5).

   A 14-ounce can of Tast-E Pop sells for $1.10, and an 8-ounce mini-can sells for $0.80. The larger can is the better value at $0.08 per ounce ($1.10 ÷ 14), while the mini-can is $0.10 per ounce ($0.80 ÷ 8).

Materials
- ☒ newspaper advertising sections
- ☒ calculators
- ☒ scissors
- ☒ glue sticks
- ☒ learning logs or lined paper

2. Invite students to find and clip out of the paper at least three ads for a product they or their families are likely to buy (e.g., three different ads for the same brand or type of cereal).

3. Have students figure out the cost per item or unit cost for each item on their list. They may need to use calculators.

4. Ask students to determine which ad offers the best deal (students can compare unit prices).

5. Have students glue their ads in their learning logs or to a piece of paper, record their price calculations next to each item, and write a summary of what they discovered. Then they can write about how they might apply what they learned to their next trip to the store with their families.

6. If time allows, have students repeat the exercise with a different product.

CRITICAL THINKING QUESTIONS

? How do advertisers use numbers to make it seem like you are getting a good deal?

? In what ways are numbers used to make the deal seem better than it really is?

PLAN A PARTY!

Students plan for and calculate the cost of hosting a party by finding services and products from the classified ads and other ads in the paper.

What to Do

1) Ask students to brainstorm items they might need to plan a celebration or party using the following categories: food, decorations, games, activities, and equipment.

2) Distribute the Plan a Party! reproducible and newspapers. (To make the activity more concrete, you can substitute a large sheet of paper for the reproducible: Have students divide the paper into six sections, labeling five of them with the categories listed in step 1. Students can cut and paste ads for items or services they want into the appropriate category spaces and use the space to calculate the cost for 20 people. They can use the sixth section to tally their grand total.)

3) Using the reproducible as a guide, students select products and services for each category and find products from the classified section and other ads to plan a party.

4) Students add up costs to determine the total cost of their event.

5) You can pose challenges such as the one at the bottom of page 50, which asks students to cut their expenses in half. You might have a contest to see who can throw the least expensive party or a party with the least expensive food. By going back and revising their plans and cost estimates, students experience real-life math problem solving.

Name _____ Date _____

PLAN A PARTY!

It's your turn to host a party! Find ads in the newspaper for services and products that will help you plan and prepare a party for 20 friends. As you locate items or services that you can use, write the name and cost in the spaces below. Try to find a theme for your party, like a birthday, Halloween, or a holiday. Parties can be planned to celebrate almost anything— like snow, sports, art, or another culture.

Party Theme: _____

Decorations: Look for ads for decorations such as balloons, flowers, or objects that relate to your theme.

Item/Service	Cost	X Amount Needed	=	Total Cost
_____	_____	X _____	=	_____
_____	_____	X _____	=	_____
_____	_____	X _____	=	_____
_____	_____	X _____	=	_____

Decorations Total = _____

Food: Look for ads that offer the right taste treats for your special event.

Item/Service	Cost	X Amount Needed	=	Total Cost
_____	_____	X _____	=	_____
_____	_____	X _____	=	_____
_____	_____	X _____	=	_____
_____	_____	X _____	=	_____

Food Total = _____

Name _____   Date _____

Games and Activities: Look for ads for games, music, and toys that will keep your guests entertained. How about buying your favorite board game or hiring a band?

Item/Service	Cost	X	Amount Needed	=	Total Cost
_____	_____	X	_____	=	_____
_____	_____	X	_____	=	_____
_____	_____	X	_____	=	_____
_____	_____	X	_____	=	_____

Games and Activities Total = _____

Equipment: What will you need to carry off the activities? Look for ads that go with your theme. How about a tent, trampoline, stereo equipment, or outdoor grill?

Item/Service	Cost	X	Amount Needed	=	Total Cost
_____	_____	X	_____	=	_____
_____	_____	X	_____	=	_____
_____	_____	X	_____	=	_____
_____	_____	X	_____	=	_____

Equipment Total = _____

Grand Total: Use your ads to estimate the total cost of your party.

_____ + _____ + _____ + _____ = _____
Decorations   Food   Games and   Equipment   Grand Total
                         Activities

. . . .
CHALLENGE
. . . .

You need to lower your expenses by 50%. What items would you delete from your list? Add the cost of these items until your original expenses are cut by 50%. Show math work in your learning log or on a separate sheet of paper.

Getting the Most Out of Teaching With Newspapers Scholastic Professional Books

WEATHER WISE

Students learn to read weather maps and practice oral communication.

What to Do

1. Using an overhead transparency, present a weather map from the newspaper. Draw on questions and terms from the Weather Wise Questions reproducible as a guide to help students accurately read the weather map. Display political and topographic maps of the United States to help students identify unlabeled places and geographic features on the weather map.

2. Distribute copies of Weather Wise Questions and have students answer the questions using the same weather map.

3. After they have answered the questions, review the answers.

4. Challenge small groups of students to use what they learned from reading the weather map to script a weather forecast. Using a transparency of their weather maps and a pointer (to simulate a TV broadcast), students can communicate temperature highs and lows in different regions, predicted amounts and types of precipitation, barometric pressures, and weather systems.

Materials

- weather map from the newspaper, 1 copy for each student
- transparency of this map
- U.S. maps (political and topographic)
- Weather Wise Questions (page 52), 1 copy for each student

EXTENSION

Local Weather Graphs

Have students keep track of the highs or lows in your area or another place of interest for several weeks. Students can then plot a line graph with the collected data.

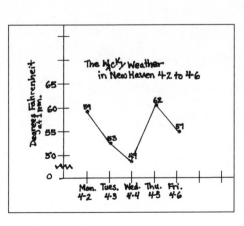

The hicky Weather in New Haven 4·2 to 4·6

51

Name _____   Date _____

WEATHER WISE QUESTIONS

Use the weather map from the newspaper to answer these questions. Keep a U.S. map handy to help you identify places and major geographic features.

1. In which states are there high-pressure areas?

_____

2. In which states are there low-pressure areas?

_____

3. How many cold fronts are there?   **4.** How many warm fronts are there?

_____   _____

5. Which states have the coldest temperatures?

_____

6. Which states have the warmest temperatures?

_____

7. Name one state where there is precipitation. What kind of precipitation is it?

_____

8. Which state or region would you like to visit, based on the weather?

_____ Why? _____

_____

9. How would you enjoy the weather there?

_____

10. Which state or region would you avoid because of weather? _____

Why? _____

BASIC NEEDS

Students locate articles that support the concept that no matter how advanced society becomes, we still rely on the same basic needs for survival.

What to Do

1. Have students identify what a wild animal needs in order to survive. (Chose an animal students are interested in or one that lives in your area.) Make a list of its needs on the board.

2. Let students categorize these items into groups. (They should come up with *food*, *water*, *shelter*, and *space*.)

3. Next ask what humans need in order to survive. Help students see how all animals have the same basic needs.

4. Distribute the Basic Needs reproducible and invite students look for articles that have a connection to our basic needs as humans (e.g., articles that focus on issues such as drought, famine relief efforts, affordable housing, and preserving wetlands). Have them use the information from the article to complete the activity page.

Materials

(for each student)
- Basic Needs (page 54)
- newspapers
- glue sticks
- scissors

CRITICAL THINKING QUESTIONS

? About which basic needs are people most concerned (which basic need appeared most frequently in the articles you found)?

? If there are problems with basic needs, which are we addressing?

? What can be done to help meet the basic needs of all people?

Name _____ Date _____

BASIC NEEDS

FOOD

HEADLINE: _____

What's the problem?

_____

What's the solution? _____

_____

WATER

HEADLINE: _____

What's the problem?

_____

What's the solution? _____

_____

SHELTER

HEADLINE: _____

What's the problem?

_____

What's the solution? _____

_____

SPACE

HEADLINE: _____

What's the problem?

_____

What's the solution? _____

_____

Getting the Most Out of Teaching With Newspapers Scholastic Professional Books

SCIENCE DISCOVERIES

Students will identify articles that feature exciting new research and discoveries in science and follow up with research on a chosen topic.

What to Do

1. Assign students to gather science-related articles.

2. Keep the collected articles posted on a bulletin board or in a scrapbook.

3. When there are enough articles, let each student pick one article that features an invention or discovery he or she wants to investigate further. Have students write to the scientist or institute involved in the project, research the topic on the Internet, or read additional newspaper articles and books about the topic.

Materials

☐ newspapers (science section, if available)

EXTENSION

"And I was there..."

After researching a discovery, students write an "And I was there..." story their learning logs. This can be a first-person account of the discovery in which students imagine that they are at the site of the discovery and give the account of the discovery based on the facts they have collected. Encourage them to illustrate a border for the account.

PART THREE

CREATING CLASS NEWSPAPERS

Creating a class newspaper is a wonderful way to combine student talents and practice important skills. Students learn to work cooperatively while planning, organizing, writing, editing, and discussing their paper in progress. Both students and teachers reap rewards when the finished product is hot off the press in the hands of an eager reader!

Quick Tips: *Making the newspaper a class effort*

Let students do most of the work. Too often, teachers take over many of the tasks in a newspaper-making project—typing and editing, doing layout, and stapling pages together. Such a teacher-directed approach not only makes the teacher unwilling to do more than a couple of issues, it also lessens the students' sense of ownership and feeling of accomplishment when the paper is finished. Giving students a greater sense of ownership will keep them motivated to continue working on the paper.

DECIDING ON A PURPOSE

Involve students in the planning stages to maximize their investment in the project. Ask the following kinds of questions: What topics should we report on? Who will our audience be? Should we include photographs? What sections should we include? What kind of advertisements could we include? What else could be in our paper? How big should it be? What kind of paper should it be printed on? What the students decide initially may be modified as the actual process is underway. Have conference sessions to discuss changes to the paper. This process teaches students valuable real-life planning and problem-solving skills.

NAMING THE PAPER

Brainstorming a list of names provides a perfect opportunity to take a class vote. Record students' suggestions on the board and have students write their favorite choice on a slip of paper. The winning name becomes the flag for the class paper.

MAKING ASSIGNMENTS

Once the newspaper's purpose and content have been decided on, students will be eager to get started. Decide what kinds of assignments are necessary to produce the paper and how many students will be needed to accomplish them. Here is a sample of how the assignments might look for a typical class newspaper.

Job	Number of Students	Job	Number of Students
reporters	5	graphic illustrators	2
feature writers	3	cartoonists	2
sports writers	2	advertisers	2
photographers	2	copy editors	4
reviewers	2	production editors	5
op-ed writers	2	layout	4

List the jobs on the board and let students write on a slip of paper two or three that they think they would like to try so that you are able to assign students one of their choices. By rotating assignments and encouraging students to take on several jobs at a time, students get a chance to experience different responsibilities and learn different skills with each issue.

USING TECHNOLOGY TO GATHER INFORMATION AND PUBLISH

E-mail: E-mail offers exciting possibilities for collecting information. For instance, when they write a book review, students can now ask questions or conduct interviews with their favorite author, or they can ask an expert for facts to support an opinion when they write an editorial.

Desktop Publishing: Students have been making class newspapers since long before computers were available in schools. There is nothing wrong with the cut-and-paste technique for producing a paper. Today's technology, however, offers more choices for how the final paper is designed and it encourages students to learn computer skills that are important and necessary. Computer applications help to display students' efforts in a polished, final edition. Many word-processing programs provide options to help create columns and spacing. Digital photographs can be used or photographs and illustrations can be scanned and inserted into the paper. Text size and fonts are easy to adjust to make writing appear as it would in published newspapers. Making adjustments to the final copy and inserting last-minute edits—just as a production manager does with a real newspaper—simulate a real newspaper production experience!

Student Newspapers on the Net: Students enjoy seeing other classes engaged in newspaper writing. Student-created newspapers are available on the Internet. Also, electronic papers often welcome student submissions. You might consider publishing your own paper on the Internet. Start with a classroom home page and take off from there. Here are two sites for students to check out.

Kid News
http://kidnews.com
This site offers a free electronic newspaper written by students from around the world. Students may submit their work to Kid News.

Kids Courier
http://kidscourier.com
This is another excellent site that features a newspaper for kids and includes opportunities for submissions.

Newspaper Assignments

Job Descriptions & Related Activities

Before you make assignments, make sure students are familiar with the different sections of the paper and the purposes of different kinds of writing. They should understand, for example, how a hard news story differs from an editorial. Short mini-lessons on the type of writing, editing, or other work that is expected for each assignment should precede the division of tasks.

As students begin independent work, it is critical that you provide good examples of work characteristic of each field: Class reporters should have access to hard news stories, editorial cartoonists should review powerful cartoons, designers should have access to graphs and charts from different sections of the paper, and so forth.

Staff Reporters: These reporters gather facts and write hard news stories that revolve around the happenings of the school, community events, and classroom activities (this is called their *beat*).

* *Finding topics:* Finding topics for the reporters to write about involves brainstorming sessions with the class. Prompt students to think of subjects with which they are directly involved. Provide a basket or drop box where students can contribute ideas that come up at other times. Subjects might include a new staff member at school, concerts and school programs, assemblies, field trips, special class events, new school equipment, or special student awards.

* *Interviews:* Teach students good interview techniques. Explain that interviews help reporters get inside information and make their articles more interesting and informative. Have students decide whom they could interview to get additional information for a story. Then have reporters write out their questions, making sure what they ask relates to the subject and can be answered with more than a yes or no response.

* *Writing Articles:* Reporters need to organize their information so that the important facts are written as leads to the articles. Emphasize note-taking with a 5 W's organizer. Explain how direct quotations can be taken from interviews to make the articles more interesting.

Feature Writers: Besides the main hard news stories, classroom papers should offer articles about other high-interest topics, such as recipes for healthy snacks, skateboard tricks, favorite television shows, new toys, or the best Internet sites for kids. Help students organize their ideas with a heading, body of information, and conclusion. Show students how surveys and interviews can be used to add information and appeal to their articles.

Photographers: Photographs add interest and a visual perspective on a story. Help your photographers decide which articles would most benefit from a photograph. Have students plan their photos, deciding what shot best illustrates the topic of the article. When photos have been developed, have students choose their best pictures and write accompanying cutlines.

Graphic Illustrators: Students put information into charts and graphs to help readers better understand collected data. These students may also create drawings to illustrate articles that don't have photographs and choose clip art to add flair to the finished paper.

Reviewers: Students write reviews of their favorite books or movies. These are short pieces and work well for a student who is a less sophisticated writer. Allow students to include reviews of favorite video games and Internet sites.

Op-Ed Writers: Students put their persuavive writing skills to use in a real-world format. Let students write their opinions on relevant subjects like school dress code or local issues. Support your op-ed writers by posting a class-generated list of possible topics (you might brainstorm topics every few days). Help students write successful editorials with these guidelines: 1) Support your opinions with facts; 2) Do not criticize individual people (state what you think is wrong with an idea instead); 3) If you believe that something should be changed, suggest ideas to make it better; 4) Include an introduction, body, and summary in your article.

Editorial Cartoonists: Have students think of humorous situations that would be fun to illustrate. Students should read other comics to see how balloons and pictures are arranged to show a humorous situation. Make copies of blank strips divided into four or five boxes. Remind students to save enough space to print their words. Finished comics should be dark enough to be copied.

Advertisers: As described in the Design an Ad extension (page 19), students can learn about the world and language of advertising by creating their own advertisements. Invite advertisers to create classified ads for actual events in your school community such as garage sales, kitten give-aways, and other parent-approved events and items.

Copy Editors: Copy editors have the important job of checking over other students' work before it is typed for the final paper. Have these students sit together so they can ask one another questions about content, spelling, and grammar. Provide their area with spell checkers, dictionaries, and three baskets labeled, "In," "Return," and "Go." Material ready for editing is put in the "In" basket. Editors check the articles carefully. If there are questions about meaning, editors write comments on the articles and place them in the "Return" basket where the authors pick them up for revision. Otherwise, the editors fix spelling and punctuation, and the finished work is placed in the "Go" basket. Students may need guidance on how to accept and give editing suggestions. Allowing all students a turn at this job helps them to be neither too critical nor too sensitive in the area of editing.

Production Editors: Typing and layout are the final jobs of building a newspaper. Students who are finished with their assignments may do the typing. Editors can also type as they wait for other incoming articles. Students enjoy typing more when they are typing other students' articles. In this way they also become familiar with classmates' writing styles and learn about stories on which others have been working. Both layout and typing can be done as a cut-and-paste process where photocopies are made of the formatted sheets. If possible, complete the paper on the computer with a word-processing program such as KidPix that allows students to cut, paste, and insert articles, photos, and illustrations.

HALFWAY THERE: CHECKUP

About halfway through the newspaper project is a great time to create a class checklist of assignments that need to be accomplished so that the class newspaper can be completed. This activity helps students keep on task, rewards them for work already executed, and gives them a clear view of their project and of what still needs to be done.

What to Do

1. With the class, brainstorm a list of all the jobs that need to be completed to make the newspaper a finished product.

2. When the list is complete, have students create the checklist poster. Ask for volunteers to write on the poster board the tasks from the brainstorm list.

3. When all students have had the opportunity to add to the poster, go over the checklist to make sure that all of the items necessary for completion are listed. If items have been left out, add them in at this time.

4. As a class, place star stickers in the spaces of those jobs that have already been completed. (As they finish the remaining tasks, students should show their completed work to you before placing a star in the box on the poster that indicates completion for that task.)

5. Hang the poster in the front of the class so that each day you can review what has been done and what still needs to be done to finish the newspaper.

Materials

- large poster board (you may need 2) on which you have created a grid to list tasks for paper completion and boxes to check when the tasks are done
- markers
- class-generated list of tasks necessary for paper completion
- star stickers

WRAP-UP: PROJECTS WITH LEFTOVER NEWSPAPERS

Now that your students are using newspapers on a regular basis, your paper-clad classroom may start to look and feel like a huge portion of fish and chips. Never fear. Newspapers can be put to good use with some of these recycling ideas.

- Use newspapers as backgrounds on bulletin boards (perfect for a current events theme!).

- Fold newspapers to make book covers.

- Tear newspapers into strips and weave to make mats. Place the mats in sealable plastic bags to create light and easy-to-carry outdoor seats.

- Use newspaper strips for papier-mâché projects.

- Crumple and use newspaper sheets as stuffing for paper sculptures.

- Roll newspaper sections into tubes to use for 3-D construction projects.

- Use pieces of newsprint with other media for collages.

- Cover and protect tables and desks with leftover newspapers when doing messy projects.

- Fold newspapers into paper hats or origami creations.

- Use the paper to create kites or paper airplanes. (See the Web Link below.)

- Recycle used newspapers in a lesson that teaches the importance of ecologically sound living.

WEB LINK: Clem's Homemade Newspaper Kite Plans

http://www.clem.freeserve.co.uk
Check out this great site, which includes plans on how to use newspapers to build a kite, as well as photographs of the kite in action, and E-mail from readers around the world who share their newspaper kite experiences. Students love this!

NEWSPAPER GLOSSARY

Banner a headline that runs across the whole page

Boldface dark, thick letters used in headlines

Break first news of an event

Byline name of news writer at the beginning of an article

Classified ads a section of the paper listing jobs and things to sell

Columnist a writer who writes regularly in the paper

Copy all printed parts of the paper

Copy desk the area in the newsroom where editors work

Copy editor someone who proofreads and edits the newspaper before the final copy goes to print

Correspondent reporter who works out of town

Cover to write the facts into a news story

Crop to cut a photograph to fit into a given space

Cut to shorten a story

Cutline a caption under a photo explaining what it is about

Dateline a heading that tells where and when the story takes place

Deadline the time when all stories and copy are due for an edition

Dummy a model copy of the paper to show where articles, ads, and pictures are arranged

Ear upper corners of the paper that give information about the section or the weather

Edit to check copy for mistakes and make it ready to print

Editor someone who assigns reporters, decides what stories should be included, organizes the paper, and improves copy

Editorial an article that tells the opinion of the writer

Feature an interesting article, not always important news

Filler a short article to fill space, not an important news item

Flag the newspaper's name printed across the top of the front page

Gutter the space along the crease where the pages fold

Hard news important news articles found on the front pages

Headline the title of an article printed in boldface

Index a list that tells where things are in the paper

Jump to continue a story on another page

Kill to remove a story before printing the paper

Layout the organization of the pictures, ads, and articles on a dummy

Lead the first few sentences that tell the 5 W's of a news story

Masthead information about the editors usually found in a box on the editorial page

Morgue a collection of the newspaper's published pictures and stories

Proof a final copy of the paper to be checked before printing

Release inside information given to the paper for an article

Reporter someone who finds facts and writes articles for the paper

Scoop an important news story that one reporter learns about first

Syndicated features columns, comics, and news stories that are sold to many newspapers

Wire service provider of news stories sent electronically to a newspaper

RESOURCES

LITERATURE CONNECTIONS

The Landry News by Andrew Clements (Simon & Schuster, 1999)

Girl Reporter Blows Lid Off Town by Linda Ellerbee (HarperCollins, 2000)

Karen's Newspaper by Ann Martin (Scholastic, 1993)

Some Good News by Cynthia Rylant (Simon & Schuster, 1999)

Joseph Pulitzer and the New York World by Nancy Whitelaw (Morgan Reynolds, 1999)

REFERENCE BOOKS

Create Your Own Class Newspaper! A Complete Guide for Planning, Writing, and Publishing a Newspaper by Diane Crosby (Incentive Publishing, 1999)

Writers Express Dave Kemper, Ruth Nathan, and Patrick Sebranek (Write Source, 1995)

Using the Newspaper to Teach ESL Learners by Rafael A. Olivares (International Reading Association, 1993)

ORGANIZATION

National Council for the Social Studies
http://www.socialstudies.org

WEB SITES

Classroom Newspaper Workshop
http://kidnews.com

Clem's Homemade Newspaper Kite Plans
http://www.clem.freeserve.co.uk/page4.html

Kids Courier
http://kidscourier.com

Kid News
http://kidnews.com

New York Times on the Web: Connections for students, teachers, and parents
http://www.nytimes.com/learning

Atlapedia Online
http://www.atlapedia.com/index.html

Use the News: Teaching Resources for Newspapers and Educators
http://usethenews.com

The Virtual Newspaper
http://www.refdesk.com/paper.html